a special gift for

_____

_____

with love,

_____

_____

date

I dedicate this book to my husband, *Ryan*,
and my son, *Asa*.
Thank you for being patient and loving
as I continue the process of being
the best mom I can be.
I love you!

Stories, sayings, and Scriptures to Encourage and Inspire the ...

hugs™

for
new
moms

STEPHANIE HOWARD
Personalized Scriptures by
LEANN WEISS

HOWARD
PUBLISHING CO.

Our purpose at Howard Publishing is to:

- *Increase faith* in the hearts of growing Christians
- *Inspire holiness* in the lives of believers
- *Instill hope* in the hearts of struggling people everywhere

Because He's coming again!

Hugs for New Moms © 2002 by Stephanie Howard
All rights reserved. Printed in the United States of America

Published by Howard Publishing Co., Inc.,
3117 North 7th Street, West Monroe, LA 71291-2227

03 04 05 06 07 08 09 10 11   10 9 8

Paraphrased Scriptures © 2001 LeAnn Weiss, 3006 Brandywine Dr.,
Orlando, FL 32806; 407-898-4410

Edited by Philis Boultinghouse
Interior design by Stephanie Denney

Library of Congress Cataloging-in-Publication Data
Howard, Stephanie, 1974-
   Hugs for new moms : stories, sayings, and Scriptures to encourage and
  inspire the—[heart] / Stephanie Howard ; personalized Scriptures by
  LeAnn Weiss.
     p. cm.
   On t.p., "[heart]" appears as a heart.
   ISBN 1-58229-223-X
   1. Mothers—Religious life. 2. Pregnant women—Religious life.
  3. Motherhood—Religious aspects—Christianity. I. Weiss, LeAnn. II.
  Title.

BV4529.18.L96 2002
242'.6431—dc21

                                  2001051518

Scripture quotations taken from the Holy Bible, New International Ver-
sion, Copyright © 1973, 1978, 1984 International Bible Society. Used by
permission of Zondervan Bible Publishers.

contents

Ten Things I Learned My First Year of Motherhood

1. When you bring the baby home from the hospital, make sure you have colic medicine.

2. The moment you sit down to eat a quiet meal, the baby *will* wake up!

3. Put away your wardrobe of "dry-clean only" outfits... indefinitely.

4. Babies enjoy the box just as much (or more) as the expensive toy inside.

5. Safety plugs are not childproof.

6. Babies know a lot more than we think they do.

7. Baby teeth hurt!

8. If you don't hold the baby properly, even a lightweight can do damage to your back.

9. Don't forget to take time for yourself.

10. Savor every moment because babies grow up way too fast!

chapter 1

a new mom's
song

I'll bless you and multiply your family,

keeping My covenant of *love* with you.

Don't let anxiety steal your *joy;*

rather, tell Me about your worries

and needs and *thank* Me in advance.

As you pray, you'll find that

My incomparable *peace* overshadows

all of your problems and insecurities.

*A*lways be **content** with what you have,
knowing that I'll never leave or abandon you.
I'll *supply* everything you need,
according to My endless **riches** in *glory.*

Faithfully providing,
Your Prince of Peace

—from Deuteronomy 7:12–13; John 16:33; Philippians 4:6–7;
Hebrews 13:5; Philippians 4:19

Most mothers have a favorite lullaby they sing to their newborns to help them fall asleep. It may be the traditional "Rock-a-Bye-Baby" or maybe just a sweet love song that seems to fit the feelings she has for her baby. Sleep specialists suggest two reasons that mothers should sing to their infants even if they can't carry a tune. First, most babies are soothed by a routine that helps them relax and unwind. Also, a quiet song in a familiar voice makes babies feel safe and calm.

Your baby has listened to you from inside the womb ever since she could hear. She heard you laugh, cry, hum, and whistle. When she entered the world, she heard your moans of exertion and your cry of exhilaration. When being pushed from a warm, dark womb to a cold, bright room, the only thing familiar to your baby was the sound of your voice. Did she care whether you were soprano or alto or something else altogether? Nope. All that mattered was the security and comfort your familiar voice provided.

With the passing of time will come many changes, but one thing will remain the same: Your child will always strain to hear your voice over the chaos of life. When struggles come, your voice will be the one she searches for.

So the next time you sing to your baby, remember: Your voice is the unique melody that opens windows of comfort and love.

When we release our children into the Father's hands and acknowledge that He is in control of their lives and ours, both we and our children will have greater peace.

—Stormie Omartian

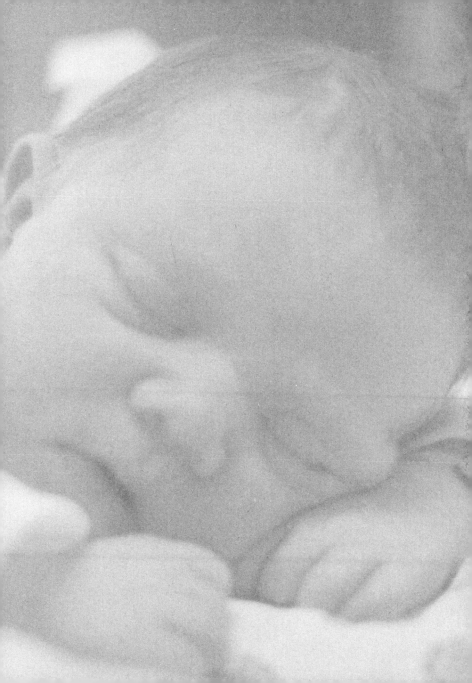

Photo by Sheryl Weaver

lisa's lullaby

He says, 'Peace, peace, be still'…" Lisa's favorite church song had been the lullaby she sang to rock her son to sleep ever since she brought him home from the hospital. Although it wasn't a typical lullaby, the calming effect the song had on her as she thought of her Savior also helped her little one drift off into a peaceful sleep. *"Like a child, the waves obey Him, when He says, 'Peace be still.'"* She gently placed eight-month-old Bryson into his crib and quietly closed the door as she left his room.

Lisa entered the living room of their small apartment where her husband, Jeremy, was focusing intently on the pile of bills in front of him. "Lisa, I don't know where it's going to come from, but we have at least eleven hundred dollars due at the end of this month! Bryson's childcare and two car notes are killing us!"

Lisa cringed as feelings of tension replaced the peacefulness she'd possessed before entering the room. Jeremy had been brooding for a week about their financial situation, and Lisa knew better than to offer any solutions at the moment.

Jeremy and Lisa had been married almost two years, and Lisa thought that by now they should have cleared the "newlywed" hurdles. She had married Jeremy despite her parents' disapproval. Whether her parents objected more to his rough "bad-boy" appearance or his lack of college education was debatable, but one thing was sure: He was not good enough for their daughter.

Lisa had been able to see through Jeremy's rough exterior to the easygoing, caring man he could be. Despite the angry words and ugly arguments between

Jeremy and her parents, she had continued to love him. After dating him only a few months, Lisa quit college and they eloped. She had known that things could be difficult at the beginning of a marriage, but she wasn't prepared for how hard married life had been.

While Jeremy made an average income working nights driving an ambulance as an emergency medical technician, Lisa made only a little more than minimum wage working at a flower shop. They barely made enough to cover expenses and had nothing left for emergencies. During the first few months, they told friends they were "living on love," which was evidenced three months after their wedding day when Lisa found out she was pregnant. And while Lisa and Jeremy had felt the excitement of having a baby, there was a strong undercurrent of fear and worry about how they would handle the added expenses and workload. Since Bryson's birth, Jeremy and Lisa's marriage had suffered, to say the least. The newlyweds argued about money, about child rearing, and most of all, about in-laws.

"I don't want your parents over here telling me what to do!" Jeremy forcefully reiterated every time Lisa had asked to invite them to their apartment. "If they don't think I'm good enough for you, I'm sure I won't be good enough for Bryson either!"

Although Lisa's parents lived across town, they had seen their grandchild only on a handful of occasions. Lisa prayed often that someday soon pride would melt, that the past would be forgiven, and that relationships could be mended for the sake of Bryson.

Lisa stood over Jeremy as he stared at the small mountain of paper, biting her lip to hold back the words she was unsure of how to say. But the words came anyway: "My parents would love to help us. We could pay them back after we get on our feet."

Lisa immediately knew she should have bitten harder. Jeremy stood up, angrily pushing his chair out of the way. "Over my dead body, Lisa! There is no way you're going to catch me groveling to your parents after the way they've treated me. Oh, I'm sure they'd love to help just so they can say 'I told you so.'" Jeremy grabbed his jacket and headed for the front door. "If you want your mommy and daddy so much, why don't you just go back home!" Jeremy slammed the door as he headed to his car to go to work.

Lisa stood motionless, staring at the door. It took a moment for Bryson's startled cries to pierce her consciousness.

Rushing to her crying baby, she scooped him up and held him close. His warm body comforted her as much as she comforted him. After soothing Bryson back to sleep, Lisa paced around the living room trying to sort out what was going on with her marriage. *This is not the way I expected my life to be! What happened to all my dreams of having a wonderful marriage and a fun, happy family? I never expected the white picket fence or that we'd have lots of money, but I always knew we'd have a lot of love. Now I feel as if I've lost my parents and my husband!* All of a sudden an overwhelming feeling of exhaustion and defeat overtook her, and she erupted in trembling sobs that shook her whole body.

Jeremy attempted to concentrate at work, but his emotions were also in turmoil. He didn't know what had gotten into him that made him talk to Lisa the way he had. All he wanted was to provide for his family and prove to Lisa's parents that he was worthy of caring for their daughter and grandson. Sure, they recently seemed to be trying to accept Jeremy as a son-in-law, but the many angry words from the past had left deep wounds that Jeremy couldn't seem to get over. Every time he thought about Lisa's parents, he couldn't help feeling judged and inadequate.

Jeremy's thoughts were suddenly interrupted by a call. Emergency assistance was needed two miles away—a one-vehicle accident and a victim with possible cardiac arrest. Jeremy jumped into the ambulance with his crew and drove quickly toward the scene of the accident. He knew that the sooner they got there, the better chance they had to save the victim. Pulling up behind the smoking vehicle, Jeremy immediately recognized the panic-stricken face of Mary, his mother-in-law. She was outside the car, leaning over the body on the driver's side. When she saw the ambulance, she yelled for them to hurry. Jeremy jumped from the ambulance with his first-aid kit and ran to the vehicle. Mary tried to speak between gasping breaths, "Phil was driving when, all of a sudden, he grabbed his chest in pain. We swerved off the road and hit the side rail; now he's unconscious. Jeremy, please do something!" Jeremy was already administering CPR and yelling at his partner to get the defibrillator to jump-start Phil's heart. The next few minutes seemed an eternity, but Jeremy finally felt Phil's pulse and heard his stabilized breathing. Phil was carried onto the ambulance, and Mary climbed in with him. Jeremy called Lisa on his cell phone as he drove her parents to the nearest hospital.

After Phil had been admitted, Mary caught up

with Jeremy as he passed through the automatic doors leading into the lobby. "Jeremy, I want to thank you for everything you did tonight. If you hadn't been there, Phil might not have made it."

Jeremy looked away, not able to make eye contact. "I was just doing my job." Once again, he turned toward the exit; but Mary grabbed his arm, turning him toward her.

"You did a good job, Jeremy. I'm proud that you are my son-in-law, and I'm glad you were there," she said sincerely, giving him a heartfelt embrace.

Jeremy smiled sheepishly. "Thanks, Mary. I'll let Lisa know that Phil is doing OK."

Once more he turned to leave, but this time Mary took hold of his hand. "Jeremy, I know we didn't start out on the best of terms, but Phil and I would like to start over, if that's all right with you."

For the first time, Jeremy saw his mother-in-law with different eyes. For some reason he didn't feel the condescending look or the judgmental air. "Yes, I'd like that…and I know Bryson would too."

One week after the accident, Lisa had to pinch herself to believe that her husband and son were laughing and playing in the same room with her parents. Although there was some hesitancy in the air, everyone was really trying to forgive the past and move toward mending relationships. *One step at a time.* Lisa smiled to herself. *This is the beginning of something wonderful!*

That night as Lisa put Bryson to bed, she sang her lullaby as she had so many times before. *"He says, 'Peace, peace, be still'…"* But tonight her song meant so much more as she envisioned her family full of peace…and joy.

a new mom's song

What song do you sing to get your baby to sleep? What
feelings or memories are associated with that song?

_____

_____

_____

_____

_____

_____

_____

_____

_____

_____

_____

_____

_____

_____

_____

a new mom's job

*W*hen motherhood
is draining the *best* of you
and you feel overwhelmed and
ill-equipped for the *responsibilities*
of caring for your family,
look up and remember
that I'm your *ever-present* helper!

*C*ome to Me, and I'll refresh you
and *recharge* your emotional,
physical, and spiritual batteries.
You'll find that with My help
you can accomplish *amazing* things
you could never do alone.

Energizing you,
Your All-Powerful God

—from Psalm 121:1-2; Matthew 11:28; Philippians 4:13

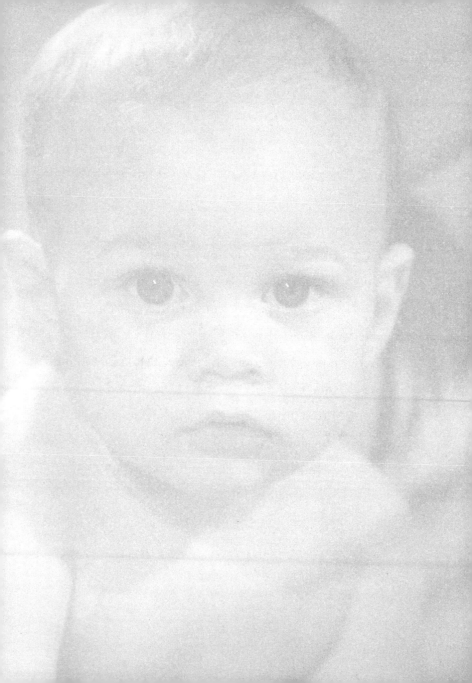

Hi, Mommy!... Yes, I'm talking to you. Oh, you aren't used to that yet, are you? Well, it won't be long."

Sure, right now you may only know the high-pitched squall of your tiny newborn as he tries to have all his little needs met. Your infant's cries for food, a clean diaper, or comfort may at times sound deafening, but if you listen carefully you may hear your name through all the noise. "Mama, hold me!" "Mama, feed me!" "Mama! I need you!"

Your little one may not be spouting off full sentences yet, but all too soon your sweet angel will have a full vocabulary that will include all those needs and more. But don't be in too much of a hurry to pass through this phase of hourly diaper changes and middle-of-the-night feedings.

Although you may feel tired, overworked, and unappreciated, you are blessed. You have been given the wonderful responsibility of caring for a child. You will be the one he goes to when he scrapes his knee. You will be the one he asks to read him his favorite story. You will be the one he says makes the best spaghetti.

His needs are so many right now, and your job is a difficult one. But make an effort to cherish every moment of this stage of helplessness and inno-cence. Because very soon you'll forget those sleepless nights and you'll forget what life was ever like before becoming "Mommy."

We have only this moment,
sparkling like a star in our hand...
and melting like a snowflake.
Let us use it before it is too late.

~Marie Benyon Ray

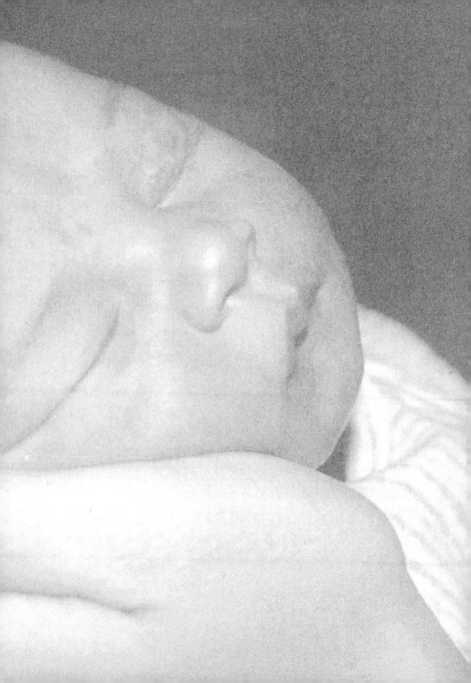

no experience necessary

I'm not cut out for this!" Susan crumpled into the recliner with her newborn son of two weeks wailing inconsolably. It was almost noon, and Susan hadn't had a chance to take a shower, eat breakfast, or even wash her face. She was still so sore from her eighteen-hour delivery (which was nothing like they had described in her childbirth classes) that she couldn't walk normally. Her breasts ached, and nursing was not going as smoothly as she had hoped. When Susan saw her reflection in the mirror, she was terribly disappointed to see that she looked far better pregnant than she did right now. Besides being totally exhausted and feeling like a complete failure for not being able to take care of the household chores, she was an emotional wreck! *How do other women do this?*

Susan sobbed as she rocked her colicky baby, remembering all her unrealistic expectations about how things would be when she became a mother. *I was so anxious for Adam to be born, but now that he's here, I'm not so sure about this "motherhood" thing. I can't even keep up with the laundry and dishes, much less care for my son! I was much better as a professional than I am as a mother!* Over the sound of her baby's cries, she called out in desperation, "Dear Lord, I can't do this! I'm not equipped to take care of this new responsibility. It's too difficult. I don't know what to do! Please help me!"

Susan was thinking of ways to send her son back where he'd come from when she heard the telephone ring. "Hello?" Susan cried into the receiver over her screaming baby.

"Susan? Are you two all right over there?"

Oh great, just what I need! If my mother-in-law has ever suspected that I can't take care of her son, now she'll know for certain that I'm incompetent to care for her grandson!

"Um, hi, Judy… Well, it hasn't been a great morning so far… I've already tried the colic medicine, he won't nurse, he won't sleep, and he won't stop crying!… Yes, I guess I've been crying too. It's just that I'm so tired!" Susan broke down once more, trying to muffle the sound of her sobs in the baby's blanket.

"I'll be right over," Judy said just before she hung up the phone.

Although it was sometimes difficult to live in the same town as her in-laws, right now Susan was extremely grateful that she did. Judy arrived in less than ten minutes to relieve Susan for a while. "Now you just go rest and don't worry about Adam and me."

"What will you do if he starts to cry again?" Susan asked, feeling guilty for needing help.

"I'll just hold him and love him; we'll be just fine," Judy answered, already carrying little Adam to the nursery.

Susan finally gave in and took a long, much-needed nap. When she woke up she found her living room tidied and an appetizing snack ready to be served. "Where's Adam? Is he OK?" Susan felt the need to recover quickly so as not to inconvenience her mother-in-law any more than she already had.

"Don't worry; he's fine. He finally fell asleep," Judy said. "Now come sit down, and let's eat while we have the chance."

As they ate, Judy told story after story of her struggles as a young mother with no family around to help. "One very hectic day I left a bag of canned goods on the front porch to be collected for a church food drive." Judy laughed as she continued, "It wasn't until later that afternoon that I realized I'd sent some needy family a large bag of dirty diapers! I was so embarrassed!" They laughed as they imagined what a shock someone must have had to find that surprise. "And Adam's daddy wasn't much better than Adam is about sleeping. He had colic until he was three months old." Judy smiled as she reminisced. "It took me two years to even *think* about having another baby."

Judy showed Susan various ways to hold Adam that would help when his tummy hurt. She also gave her a list of things Susan shouldn't eat while nursing. "I had no idea that what I eat could be affecting Adam's stomach that much!" Susan exclaimed. "No wonder he cries so much after nursing!"

"It took me awhile to find out that lettuce was bothering Jason," Judy added. "And I thought I was doing good to eat healthy and lose those pregnancy pounds. Well, once I figured that one out, no more salads for six months!"

After they finished eating, Judy cleaned up the kitchen, but she had to scold Susan twice for trying to help. "Susan, I'd like to let you in on a little secret you may not be aware of." Judy sat down next to Susan, placing her hand on top of Susan's. "Every new mother feels what you are feeling. Being a mother is hard! I don't know anyone who can say that the transition from an office job to being a stay-at-home mom is a walk in the park, although I do hope you do that too—walk in the park, I mean. God has blessed you with a beautiful son. But not only that: He has blessed you with the specific talents needed to care for your whole family. Don't ever doubt that. You may not have all the answers—no one does—but you'll have the resources to get the answers you need. And don't worry about getting everything done around the house they way you did before you became a mother. It will get easier with time. Right now, your main job is to love Jason and little Adam. The dishes may not do themselves, but paper plates sure are handy!" They laughed and talked for a while longer until they heard Adam piping in from the nursery.

"Well, I guess duty calls!" Susan sighed as she got up from the kitchen table. But as she walked into the nursery and saw her sweet little man, she knew how very blessed she was to have a beautiful, healthy baby. And how very blessed she was that God had given her exactly what she needed to make it through the day.

a new mom's job

Record your own trials as a new mom. Maybe you can share them with your child when he or she has your grandchildren!

_____

_____

_____

_____

_____

_____

_____

_____

_____

_____

_____

_____

_____

_____

_____

_____

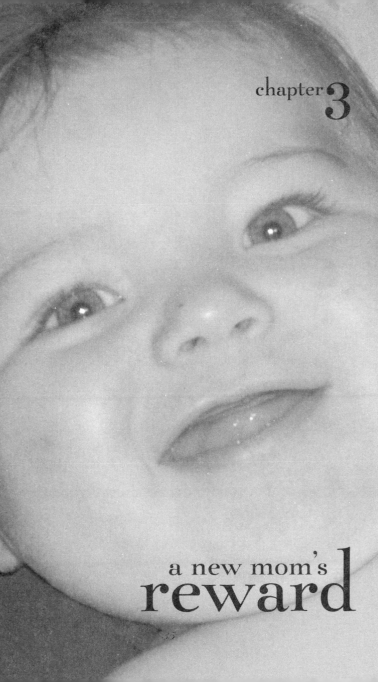

a new mom's
reward

Always remember that every
good and **perfect** gift
—including the wonder of a *newborn baby*—
is a heavenly *blessing* from Me.

$\mathcal{S}$urely My goodness
and endless *love* will enrich you
every day of your life.
You can count on My *faithfulness*
from generation to generation.

Blessings and love,
Your Heavenly Father

—from James 1:17; Psalms 23:6; 127:3; 100:5

Do you realize how much it costs to raise a child these days? A recent calculation stated that the average cost of bringing up a child from birth to age eighteen is $160,140. (That doesn't even include college tuition!) That amount translates to $8,896.67 a year, $741.39 a month, $171.09 a week, $24.37 a day, or a little more than $1 per hour. And for all the parents who had to pay thousands of dollars to adopt their babies, the amount is even higher.

Some may look at these numbers and wonder whether the return is worth the investment. But really, the rewards are priceless. Here are just a few of the benefits of being a mother: Carefree cuddles and sweet slobber kisses. Silly giggles and chubby-toe wiggles. Arms that hold you tight and sweet prayers good night. Unconditional love and a new view of God above. You'll be the prettiest mom in the world to one set of little eyes. You'll nurture a uniquely wonderful human being under your motherly intuition and guidance. Your way will be the best way—at least to one tender heart. You'll receive lessons on trust, forgiveness, and unconditional acceptance at no additional cost. You'll live with the knowledge that your investment in another life helped make the world a better, brighter place. A dollar an hour? It's worth every penny.

Blessed be childhood, which brings
down something of heaven into the midst
of our rough earthliness.

~ Henri Frederic Amiel

a reward for waiting

Carmen had been pacing back and forth from the living room to the kitchen for nearly thirty min-utes. She was trying to find something to do as she waited for the telephone to ring. After fluffing all the pillows, she had straightened and restraightened the picture frames, and now she was having a hard time finding anything else that needed doing.

"Ring!" *Finally!* she thought as she jumped to grab the phone. Carmen stood perplexed as she listened to the dial tone until she realized that it was not the telephone but the doorbell that was ringing. Before she could get to the unlocked door, her best friend, Brooke, walked right on in.

"Hey, girl! Have you heard yet?"

Carmen shook her head. "Not yet, and I'm about to go crazy!" Carmen had been trying to get pregnant for three years and, for the past six months, had undergone several different procedures to achieve pregnancy—but without success. Their latest attempt, Dr. White had said, was one of their last options. And right now Carmen was waiting for her fertility doctor to call and tell her if the procedure had worked.

Just when Carmen had decided she would call the doctor's office to find out what was taking so long, the telephone rang. "Hello?" Carmen answered. Brooke stood close by to be supportive and to get the gist of the conversation. Carmen nodded and said "Uh-huh" and "OK" several times before hanging up.

Brooke stood waiting for Carmen to say something. "Well, what did she say?"

Carmen gave a weak smile and said, "The procedure didn't work, and I'm not pregnant. I can try again in a few months, but Dr. White said my chances of getting pregnant will decrease each time we go through the process. She said it may be time to start thinking about adoption."

Not sure what to say, Brooke said what she thought would help. "I know what you must be feeling. Even though it didn't take Brian and me very long to get pregnant the first time, you may just need to try a little longer. Or maybe you need to take a break from trying for a while."

How can she say that when she's had three babies, two of which were unexpected? Carmen thought to herself.

She was staring blankly out the kitchen window when Brooke said the words that always opened up the floodgates. "Are you OK?"

Carmen could contain her emotions no longer. All the weariness of the past three years released itself through an outpouring of tears. She was tired of being jealous of her friends who had babies. Tired of being angry that life was so unfair. Tired of feeling the ache of empty arms. Carmen was tired of begging God for a child.

Brooke tried to hug her friend, but Carmen pulled away, not willing to receive the embrace of someone who truly could not understand. "I'm sorry, Brooke, but I really need to be alone right now."

Looking surprised and dejected, Brooke nodded her head and whispered, "I'll talk to you later," then left Carmen to cry alone.

When she could cry no longer, Carmen got up from the sofa and called her husband, Heath. "Hey, honey. Dr. White just called." Carmen sighed heavily before continuing. "She said it didn't work. I think it's time that we start looking into adoption."

"I'm leaving the office right now," Heath replied. "I'll be home in twenty minutes."

As Heath hurried into the house, Carmen met him with a tender kiss, letting him know just how much she appreciated his comforting presence. Stepping back, she noticed that he had one hand behind his back. "What are you hiding back there?" she asked suspiciously.

With a mischievous grin, he presented his lovely wife with a bouquet of fragrant roses in pink and lavender.

"They are so beautiful!" Carmen's eyes lit up at the sight and smell of the flowers. Heath laid the roses on the kitchen table and bent down to kiss his wife again.

"I have something to tell you," he said as he grabbed her hand and led her to the living-room sofa. Once they were both seated, Heath began. "Last week I got a call from Paul Gaskins, my old college buddy who started a medical practice in Georgia a few years ago. We've e-mailed off and on since college, and he knows we've been trying to have a baby for a long time. He told me that he has a pregnant patient who wants to give her baby up for adoption. Paul told her about us and that we could give her child a loving home. At the time, I told Paul that I wanted to wait until we found out the results of this test before we thought about adoption." Heath watched Carmen carefully as he continued his story.

"And then today Paul called again to see if we'd heard anything. He said this girl really wants to meet us now that she knows she's having twins!" Heath sat expectantly, waiting to see what Carmen thought about this new development.

Carmen held her breath as if the news were a precious bubble that she might accidentally pop. *Could it be that after so many years of wanting a little baby, I might actually get two babies?* Carmen sat still, entertaining the notion of having two little bundles to care for. Two bassinets, two infant swings, two highchairs, two of everything! She laughed at the thought and in that moment was sure that it was exactly what she wanted. She looked at Heath with a smile and said, "If you're ready to help change twice as many diapers, I'm ready to stay up twice as long in the middle of the night!"

For the next several months, Heath and Carmen flew back and forth to Georgia to meet with the young woman who was carrying their sons. Although the pregnancy had been an unexpected turn of events for the college student, she was determined not to add to her mistakes by having an abortion. She felt that the least she could do was give these babies a chance to live in a family that would need them as much as they needed a family. Heath and Carmen certainly fit the profile. And for that, all parties were grateful.

Brooke was the first to offer Carmen help in getting the nursery decorated and the house baby-proofed. Brooke was also the one to offer reassurance on those nights when Carmen doubted the babies would ever be hers.

And on that day when the babies finally arrived, Brooke was the one who planned the perfect baby shower to welcome the babies home. It was a complete success! Carmen and Heath's house was bursting at the seams, full of family and friends who had come to celebrate the beginning of this wonderful adventure. Matching outfits, baby supplies, and toys were everywhere! Carmen was truly seeing double as she surveyed all the gifts.

Having opened the last gift, she stood to thank all her loved ones. "Thank you for this wonderful shower, and thank you all for your prayers and support the past several years as Heath and I have tried to start a family." Carmen spotted Brooke on the other side of the room and choked back the hot tears that sprang to her eyes.

"I've been through some hard times when I was angry and hurt because I wanted what most of you already have." She locked eyes with Brooke and plunged ahead, "I want to say that I'm sorry for rejecting your kind intentions." Brooke returned her gaze with a sweet smile of forgiveness. Smiling broadly at the roomful of people, Carmen continued, "Words will never express the love I have for all of you. Thank you so much for everything! And I want to say a special thanks to God for the double blessing He has given me."

Everyone clapped and took turns hugging Carmen and passing around her precious baby boys. Brooke waded through the crowd to reach Carmen. Before Brooke could speak, Carmen hugged her best friend and said, "I love you, Brooke."

Brooke hugged back and said, "I love you, too, Mama. And I want you to know that no matter what, I will always be there for you."

Carmen pulled away from the hug with a mischievous grin. "Even in the middle of the night when the boys won't sleep?"

Brooke nodded. "Yes, even in the middle of the night."

Carmen smiled. "Even when the boys have fever and cry nonstop?"

Brooke nodded again. "Even when they're sick, you can call me."

Carmen lifted her eyebrows and questioned once more. "Even when they become loud, roughhousing teenagers whom I'll be tempted to send to military school?"

Brooke hesitated only for a second before answering, "Um, no, you'll have to handle those years without me. By then I'll be enjoying an empty nest somewhere in Maui!" Brooke patted Carmen on the shoulder before adding, "But don't worry, I'll reserve a spot right next-door for you. By the time you get there, you'll need it!"

Carmen laughed joyfully as she gazed in wonder at her baby boys and all the adventures that lay ahead.

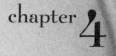
chapter 4

a new mom's
anticipation

*J*ust as sure as the sun
comes up every *morning*,
you can *trust* Me!
I've already *orchestrated* all of your days.
I *know* the plans I have for you.

*F*ollowing Me offers
you and your family
hope and a *bright future.*

In fact, I delight in superceding
your expectations and your *dreams.*

Hope-filled hugs,
Your Creator

—from Lamentations 3:23; Psalm 139:16;
Jeremiah 29:11; Ephesians 3:20

Few things in life are as exciting as the anticipation of a new baby. Your graduation, your wedding day, and of course, the day you begin life as a Christian are some of life's most exciting times. But there is a unique sense of newness and wonder that precedes the birth of a child.

When a baby is forming in your body, you wonder if she'll have her daddy's eyes or her mommy's complexion. You imagine that she'll get her grandmother's gift of music and her uncle's sense of humor. You can hardly wait to meet the little person who wriggles and pushes and kicks inside you, signaling that she can't wait to meet you either.

And isn't the wait worth it? Those long, tiresome months watching your body transform as it nurtures the growing child within are hardly remembered the moment your sweet, soft infant is placed securely in your arms. Once you feel that tiny hand wrap tightly around your finger, you know that all the time you spent planning and preparing were meant for this moment.

Yes, your heart may feel on the verge of bursting, not quite able to contain all the love you feel for this small package of a miracle; but after all, this uncontainable love is half of what you've been anticipating!

Each friend represents a world in us,
a world possibly not born until they
arrive, and it is only by this meeting
that a new world is born.

~Anaïs Nin

great expectations

W ho would have guessed that after so many years apart their friendship could have picked right back up so effortlessly!

Katelyn and Kimberly had been best friends since the fourth grade. Their friendship began when Kimberly insisted on meeting the new girl in school. And what started out as a courteous gesture became the beginning of a lifelong bond.

Since that first day of school when Katelyn had toured the school with Kimberly, they'd been inseparable. Katelyn played the piano; Kimberly sang. Kimberly liked to draw; Katelyn loved poetry. Kimberly could make the perfect lemonade for their lemonade stand, and Katelyn was the entrepreneur who handled the profits of their small enterprise. Between the two of them, there was very little they couldn't do.

One of the games they played most often revolved around planning their futures together. They had three-ring binders full of magazine cutouts of the wedding dresses they would wear at their double wedding. They included pictures of their dream cars and dream houses. They even picked out what their husbands and children would look like! Of course, they would meet their husbands at the same time, become mommies and have all their babies at the same time, and live right next-door to each other.

As time passed, however, the development of other relationships and interests crowded out the times shared between the duo. And upon high school graduation, it became clear that separate paths awaited the girls. Katelyn decided to go to a local college and married her high school sweetheart, Jeff, while Kimberly went away to a school of arts back East. After graduation, she managed to get a job as an art teacher and eventually met and married Sam, a promising, young pediatrician. For several years their only contact was e-mail and an occasional call, but they both dreamed that someday their lives would include each other.

Then early one morning, before the sun had a chance to peep through her miniblinds, Katelyn was awakened by the telephone. "Hello?" she groggily answered.

"What do you want first: the good news or the really good news?" Katelyn already knew that it was Kimberly beaming through the phone.

"What time is it?" Katelyn whispered, trying not to wake Jeff.

"I know it's early, but I just couldn't wait for Pacific time to catch up with eastern time, so just tell me which news you want first!" Kimberly insisted.

"OK," Katelyn answered, "uh, the good news, I guess."

"We're going to have a baby!" Kimberly shrieked into the telephone.

"That is so wonderful! Congratulations!" Katelyn squealed back, jumping out of bed to go where she could speak loudly. "Well, what news could be better than that?"

"Sam is going to join a medical practice right there in La Jolla!" Kimberly shrieked once more.

This news was nearly too much for Katelyn that early in the morning. "I can't believe it! It's really true, you're moving back home?"

"Yep, we'll be there in four months!" Kimberly filled her in on the details as they talked the morning away.

As the moving plans formed, the girls were giddy with the idea that they would once again be close to each other, involved in the mundane activities of each other's lives. Kimberly arrived a few weeks early to find a place to live—and, of course, she stayed with Katelyn. It didn't take long to find exactly what she wanted only a few miles from Katelyn's house. With Katelyn's help, Kimberly wasted no time in getting an appointment with the best doctor in town.

"Do you mind coming with me to my ultrasound appointment since Sam won't be here until next week?" Kimberly was trying to surprise Sam in a big way once she knew what they were having and wanted Katelyn to be there to share in the plans.

"I wouldn't miss it!" Katelyn was already brainstorming how Kimberly should announce the gender of the baby.

"Why don't we have balloons delivered to Sam's office in blue or pink?" Katelyn suggested. "Or we could e-mail him a picture of the ultrasound and let him figure it out!"

The ultrasound technician had been silent for at least a whole three minutes when she turned to the girls and said, "From the looks of it, I'm 99 percent sure that…," she paused for effect, "Kimberly is having a girl!" The two friends squealed with delight as Katelyn leaned over to give Kimberly a hug.

"Whoa! Head rush!" Katelyn felt woozy as she stood up from the hug.

"Are you all right?" Kimberly asked, still lying on the exam table.

Katelyn sat down, putting her head between her legs. "Yeah, just feeling a little dizzy all of a sudden. I must have gotten too caught up in the excitement."

Kimberly looked at Katelyn suspiciously. "Now, you're not pregnant…are you?"

Katelyn laughed at the possibility. "No…well, I don't think so."

On their drive home from the ultrasound, Kimberly giggled to herself. Katelyn turned to her friend, wondering what was so funny. Kimberly felt Katelyn's stare and blurted out, "Wouldn't it be so cool if we were pregnant at the same time?"

Katelyn coughed out her response: "What makes you think I'm pregnant?"

Kimberly patted Katelyn lightly on the shoulder. "Girl, I know the beginning signs when I see them! C'mon, let's go get a pregnancy test, just for fun." Katelyn looked like she needed a little more persuasion, so Kimberly added, "I'll buy!"

During the two-minute wait for the results of the test back at Katelyn's house, giddiness filled the girls. As they entertained the hope of their childhood fantasy coming true, giddiness turned to shock as Kimberly recognized the familiar little pink lines that were already hypnotizing Katelyn. "Well, I guess Sam won't be the only one in for a surprise today!" Katelyn laughed, now trying to decide how to tell Jeff.

So, of course, once again the friends were inseparable. It didn't hurt that Katelyn eventually found out that she would be shopping for pink as well.

As the months progressed, the expectant mothers easily slipped back into a close friendship. They shopped for baby beds together. They registered at all the baby stores together. They signed up to take their childbirth classes together (well, with their husbands, too, of course). They even picked up their old pastime of collecting magazine articles and cutouts of their favorite baby paraphernalia.

Then one afternoon, the girlfriends plopped down on Kimberly's couch to have another round at trying to name their girls. They were quite a sight. With feet propped up on the coffee table, each of the radiant young ladies cradled her own big belly, laughing till it hurt. "Hey, what about Minnie and Daisy?"

"Or how about Thelma and Louise?"

"Oh, I know, Lucy and Ethel!" Katelyn and Kimberly were having a little too much fun thinking up girl names that would depict the kind of relationship they hoped their daughters would enjoy. They couldn't help but imagine that someday their little girls would share laughs, tears, and dreams and grow up to become the best of friends.

a new mom's
hope

*N*o matter what you're up against,

always remember that I am for you!

Absolutely nothing and no one,

not even **death**, can ever

separate you from My *love.*

Don't let go of the hope you have,

for I never break My *promises* to you.

*R*einforce your hope with My Word,

knowing that every *Scripture* was written

to give you **encouragement** and hope

as you wait patiently for My *promises.*

My forever love,

Your Faithful Father

—from Romans 8:31, 35-38; Hebrews 10:23; Romans 15:4

Every mother has certain dreams for her child. Someday, he'll grow up to be a husband and father... Someday, she'll complete college... Maybe he'll find a cure for cancer... Maybe she'll help the homeless.

It is a wonderful thing to dream and plan about what the future holds for our children. And while it is good to dream about all the things they will accomplish, there is one thing that is more important: our children's souls. Each of us should be dreaming of the day when we will see our children accept Jesus into their own lives. With all the love we mothers have for our children, what greater pleasure is there than the knowledge that we will be together with them forever in heaven?

As you hold your tiny newborn in your arms, you probably aren't thinking about life beyond this earth. But that life will last an eternity, while this world is only temporary. Why not start thinking today about what you can do to help your child get to heaven? Start praying with that little one. Read the Bible to your baby. Sing songs about Jesus. Talk about God and what He has done in your family's lives. Share your dreams with others and with your children when they are older. Not only will sharing your faith encourage your child to love the Lord; it will create a legacy for future generations of dreamers. Don't ever stop dreaming!

Who could look into the eyes
of such a miracle
and doubt the reality of God?

—Angela Thomas Guffey

promise to gran-annie

Let's do lunch!" It had been "their phrase" for as long as Christi could remember. Christi had loved to "do lunch" with her favorite grandmother, Gran-Annie, ever since she was a little girl. When she was young, Christi spent almost every weekend with her grandparents, who lived only an hour away. Gran-Annie was a spry little lady with a hop in her step and a twinkle in her eye. She was an old-fashioned kind of grandmother, but not one to miss a beat. Gran-Annie could brighten any kind of day with a funny story about life in the "good old days." Christi had always loved to help Gran-Annie prepare food in the kitchen and set the table. Then they'd call Grandpa, and the three of them would enjoy a leisurely meal complete with lots of stories.

Even though it had been many years since she'd spent the weekend with her grandparents, Christi still maintained a close relationship with her seventy-eight-year-old Gran-Annie. Sure, she had a busy life with her husband, John, and her job as a corporate lawyer, but Christi made sure there was always enough room now and then to call Gran-Annie and say, "Let's do lunch!"

The past few years since her grandfather had died, Christi had shared many more lunches with Gran-Annie. It had been good for both of them to have someone to share their feelings with; Gran-Annie talked about her life as a senior, and Christi about her frustrations as a corporate woman. But today Christi had called her grandmother to lunch at a quaint family-owned deli to share some good news. "Gran-Annie, I'm going to have a baby!" Christi declared radiantly.

"Well, if that isn't the best news I've heard in weeks! And I didn't think anything better than getting my publisher's sweepstakes notification in the mail could happen today!" Gran-Annie said with a wink. "I'm so proud of you, Christi. I know you and John have been waiting for this for quite a while now. This is the beginning of a wonderful adventure for the two of you." Leaning over, she hugged her granddaughter before continuing. "Raising children can have its challenges, but the love and joy you receive far outweigh the work."

Christi shook her head in wonder. "Gran-Annie, I can't imagine your ever feeling like motherhood was a challenge! You know everything there is to know about caring for children, a husband, and a home!"

Trying not to laugh while sipping her tea, Gran-Annie set her glass down quickly. "Now, Christi, I've been around the block a few times since I began my journey into motherhood. Way back then, I struggled like every other new mother to learn how to care for a home." Christi watched as her grandmother leaned back in her chair and reminisced. "I remember a time not long after I'd delivered my third baby—your daddy—when the twins, who were barely toddlers, were into everything and I thought my life couldn't be more difficult. Come to find out, I was already expecting your Uncle Jack! Talk about a challenge; my blood pressure starts to rise just thinking about it!" They laughed out loud, drawing the attention of nearby diners who were curious about the unlikely companions—one young and poised in her navy business suit and the other weathered yet vibrant in an outdated yellow sweater.

When they finished their lunch, Christi walked her grandmother to her car. "Lunch was good, but maybe next time we can do lunch at my place. I'll fix one of my home-cooked, tried-and-true recipes," Gran-Annie said.

Christi bent down and kissed her grandmother's forehead. "Sounds like a deal to me! Good-bye, I love you!" Gran-Annie blew a kiss before backing out of the parking lot.

As the weeks progressed during her pregnancy, Christi often called her grandmother to share the details of how she was feeling and what happened at her doctor's appointments. Gran-Annie enjoyed being included in the day-to-day adventures of her granddaughter's pregnancy. "It makes me feel young again and brings back memories of my early years as a mother." Such a statement would always inspire yet another story of the "good old days."

One day Christi asked Gran-Annie to come with her to look for maternity clothes. "Let's go shopping this weekend. All my clothes are beginning to get too tight, and I don't think anyone in the courtroom wants to see buttons popping off my suit! I'll have to find some outfits that will grow with me for the next several months."

Gran-Annie thought it was a great idea and added, "After we shop we can come back to my house for lunch. There are a few things I want to talk to you about."

Saturday was a splendid spring day—ideal for shopping. After Christi had picked out several jackets and shirts she could mix and match with some basic skirts and pants, they were ready for lunch. Since the weather was so perfect, they decided to take their lunch on Gran-Annie's porch and enjoy the view overlooking a small yard with a well-groomed flower garden blooming at one end. "Oh, Gran-Annie, this has been such a perfect day! And lunch is delicious!"

Gran-Annie thanked her granddaughter for the compliment and then took on a more serious tone. "Christi, there's something I've been meaning to tell you, and it won't be easy for me to say." Christi sat quietly, having no idea what her grandmother was about to share. "Last week I went to the doctor to have a lump examined. The results show that I have a malignant tumor." Gran-Annie took Christi's hand, holding it firmly. "It has already entered my bloodstream, and the doctor says that there isn't a lot that can be done at this point."

Christi pulled her hand away to steady herself against the table. "Gran-Annie! How can this be! Surely there is something we can do!" Christi's face turned blotchy as she tried to hold back the tears, but they streamed down her face unhindered.

Gran-Annie simply shook her head. "Your mom and dad have already taken me to two other doctors, and their opinions are the same. They say I may have six months with the medicine they gave me."

Christi stood up from the table, fighting hysteria. "No! This can't be happening! I don't want you to die!" Christi began pacing back and forth, trying to think of a way to fix the situation. "There has to be something else we can do..."

Gran-Annie walked to her precious granddaughter.

"Honey, I'm too old to handle the therapies usually prescribed for cancer patients."

Upon hearing the actual word *cancer*, Christi broke into sobs. "What am I going to do without you, Gran-Annie? My baby won't even know you. I don't want to have just pictures and memories of you; I want you!"

Gran-Annie held her granddaughter, softly stroking her hair as they rocked on the porch swing. "I know, sweetheart. This is not what I had planned either. I don't know how long I'll be on this earth, but I do know one thing: I'm going to be in heaven, and I'm counting on you to help my great-grandbabies make it there too, so we can all be together someday."

They sat together in that swing for what seemed like hours as they talked and cried and made promises about how they would always cherish life and the relationships God had given them.

Spring turned to summer, and with fall came the onset of Christi's labor pains. Eight hours after

Christi's first contraction, she was staring straight into the eyes of her beautiful newborn baby. As Christi held their precious little Annie, she looked toward heaven with tears of joy and sadness. "Thank you, God, for my Annie. Help me to be the best mother I can for my daughter so she will get the chance to meet Gran-Annie in heaven someday."

a new mom's hope

**Record some precious memories of generations past
to share with your "link to the future."**

_____

_____

_____

_____

_____

_____

_____

_____

_____

_____

_____

_____

_____

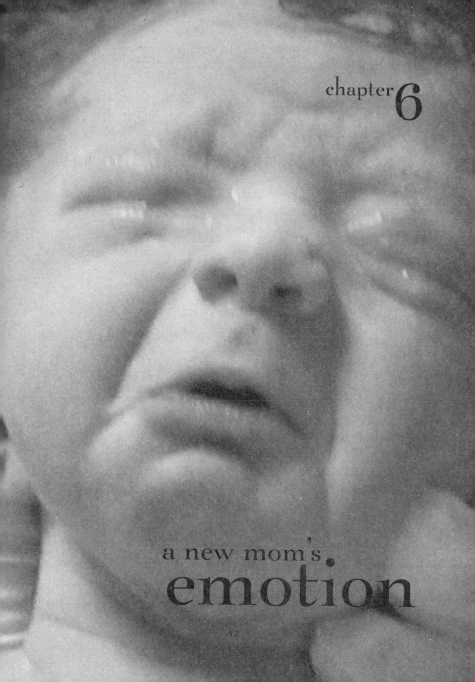

a new mom's
emotion

*A*ll things are possible with Me!
You can't even begin to *imagine*
the wonders I have waiting for you
because you *love* Me.

*A*s you trust in Me,
I'll fill you with all *joy* and *peace*
so you'll overflow with hope
by the *power* of My Holy Spirit!
May your home be *blessed*
with the continual feast of cheerful hearts.

Joyfully,
Your God of All Hope

—from Matthew 19:26; 1 Corinthians 2:9; Romans 15:13; Proverbs 15:15

What happened the moment you found out you were pregnant? Were you in total shock? Did you call everyone you knew? Did you laugh? Did you cry? The moment a woman realizes that she is carrying another life can bring an array of emotions. Some may feel excitement while others feel fear. Some women feel joy while others experience anxiety. Most women probably experience a mixture of all these emotions thanks to the surge of hormones that occurs while pregnant.

These feelings are rightly owned. From that moment of conception, your life will never again be the same. You may come to this realization with the onset of morning sickness or that first stretch mark. Or it may not hit you until the doctor places that slippery, sprawling baby on your chest. No matter when it happens, sooner or later you'll know: You have now contributed to the miracle of life; you will forever be a part of another human being. Before you give birth, your baby is sustained by your body alone. After birth, no matter where he goes, he will have part of you flowing through his veins.

No wonder we experience so many emotions when we find out we will be mothers: We have been given the opportunity to be part of a wonderful miracle! Amazing, isn't it?

We stand as a link
in a long chain of mother love,
blessed and held together by God.

—Faith B

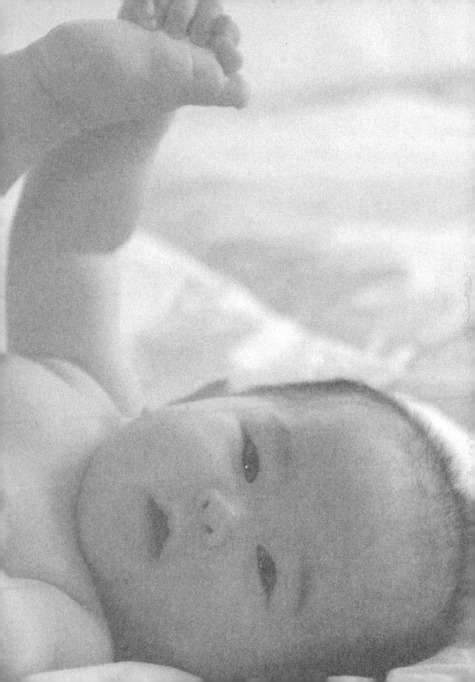

surprise blessing

Sarah Denney honked the horn for the second time. "Angie! We gotta go, or you'll be late for school!" The engine of the minivan was already humming, as Sarah waited in the driver's seat for her younger daughter to come out of the house. Her older daughter, Pam, who was sixteen going on twenty, waited patiently in the front passenger's seat reading a book. Pam was her smart, gentle, responsible daughter who didn't attract much attention as far as behavior went, but turned quite a few heads when it came to her looks. Actually, both of her daughters were very beautiful, with long, thick black hair and large, dark eyes. They took after their father, Michael, who was of American-Indian descent.

Angie appeared from the carport door. "Mom, I can't find my soccer cleats! Do you know where they are?"

"They're under the coffee table in the living room. Honey, get 'em and let's go!" Sarah's patience was wearing thin as she was tested once more by her daughter's budding adolescence. Angie was the free spirit of her two girls. At fourteen, she was generous and genuine and everyone's best friend.

Finally, Angie bustled into the minivan with backpack, gym bag, and textbooks piled high in her arms. She threw them into the backseat and slammed the sliding door shut. Angie apologized as she slid into the empty seat and fastened her seat belt. "Sorry, guys. I meant to get my things together last night, but I forgot." Angie was full of personality and fun but didn't possess the organizational skills that Pam did.

"Why don't we start packing your bags earlier in

the evening? That way we don't have to do this again," Sarah suggested.

"Hey, that's a great idea, Mom!" Angie, never one to argue, would agree to most anything. The three chatted as they drove the five miles to school.

As they pulled up to the front of Lexington High School, Angie slid the van door open and jumped out. "Now don't forget. My soccer game starts at five o'clock."

"Don't worry, baby." Sarah leaned out the window to kiss her cheek. "Dad and I will be there."

Pam grabbed her backpack and kissed her mom as well. "And remember, I have driver's education after school, so I'll just see you at the game."

Sarah put the car in drive, "Sounds like a plan. I'll see you girls this afternoon! I love you!" As she watched her girls meet up with friends and walk into the school, she planned the rest of her day. *OK. Take Michael's suits to the cleaners… Lunch with the ladies Bible class at eleven o'clock… Oh, yeah, and my appointment with Dr. Bryan at two o'clock.* Sarah had scheduled the appointment a week ago after experiencing several spells of weakness and dizziness. She was even having hot flashes and wondered if she was entering the beginning of menopause. *I'll only be forty this year, but I think early menopause runs in the family. I'll have to ask Mom later.* She pushed the idea to the back of her mind as she began her busy day.

Sarah spoke candidly with Dr. Bryan about all the symptoms she'd been experiencing. "I've been having dizzy spells and feeling really fatigued. The spells usually don't last long—they kind of come in waves. I'm also having hot flashes. I'm wondering if maybe it's early menopause."

Dr. Bryan checked her vitals and then looked over her chart. "Why don't we do some blood work and run a few tests and see what we find." While she waited, Sarah made a list of errands she still had to do before Angie's soccer game. When Dr. Bryan returned to the exam room, she was finishing her grocery list. "So, Dr. Bryan, is it menopause like I thought?" Sarah asked as she put the list in her purse.

Dr. Bryan sat down on his stool across from her. "Well, no, not exactly. I know this isn't what you are expecting to hear, but…," he studied her before finishing, "you are pregnant."

Sarah went numb, and her mouth dropped open. Then a mixture of disbelief and panic rushed through her as she questioned the doctor, "Are you sure? Can that be right? I'm almost forty years old!"

Dr. Bryan attempted to calm her with his reassuring smile. "You're most definitely pregnant; in fact, your hormone levels are so high you've probably been pregnant for a while now. I don't want to worry you, but because of your age we'll need to monitor this pregnancy a little more closely than most. In fact, we'll do an ultrasound today to determine how far along you actually are."

Sarah felt like her head was in a cloud. She wasn't sure how she was supposed to think or feel. *Is this really happening? What am I going to tell the girls? What am I going to tell Michael? I'm too old to start all over again! I did not plan to spend the next twenty years raising a child!*

The ultrasound monitor appeared much clearer than she remembered from fifteen years ago. "The technology has certainly progressed since Pam was born," Sarah mumbled to herself, waiting for the doctor to say something. Her concerns were confirmed when Dr. Bryan pointed to the little heart beating rapidly on the screen. "There really is a baby in there," Sarah admitted to herself, staring at the screen in shock.

The doctor nodded in agreement, "Yes, and it looks like you've been carrying this little guy for about eighteen weeks. Unfortunately I can't tell yet if we're looking at a 'he' or a 'she,' but we're looking at a baby who has all its fingers and toes and everything in the right place. That's all I care about at this point."

Sarah left the doctor's office unsure of where she

should go next. Without thinking, she drove to Michael's office to tell him the news. Michael was on the telephone when Sarah peeked in. He held up his hand signaling that the call shouldn't be much longer. Sarah sat down across from his desk until he hung up the phone. "Hey, sweetie, what are you doing on this side of town? I thought we were meeting at Angie's soccer game."

Sarah got up and walked around to Michael's side of the desk, putting her arms around his neck. "You know those symptoms I thought were part of early menopause?" She braced herself, unsure of how Michael would respond. "Well, it's not menopause." Sarah closed her eyes as she blurted out, "We're going to have another baby!"

Michael jumped out of his chair and took hold of her shoulders. "Are you sure?" he asked looking directly in her eyes. Unsure of the emotion behind his question, she simply nodded and handed him a picture of the ultrasound. Michael studied the picture, then hugged his wife, lifting her off her feet. "That's great, sweetie!" Michael squeezed tightly, then released her back to the floor before reaching for the office intercom. "Attention everyone! Sarah and I are having another baby!"

Perplexed, Sarah looked up at her husband, "Wait, you're not shocked, nervous, or upset?"

"Of course not! Even though this isn't what we expected, I know God has a plan for us. You're such a great mom to Pam and Angie, and I'm sure it will all work out just fine."

Although she was feeling better, it wasn't until they told the girls that she started to feel excited. "Mom, I can't believe it!" Pam said as she threw her arms around Sarah's neck.

"You go, girl!" Angie exclaimed.

Sarah questioned the girls, "So, you're really excited about having a little brother or sister to help take care of? You know that means unpaid babysitting, and you two will have to share a room."

"Aw, Mom, that doesn't matter. It will be fun to have a little one around." Angie kept talking as she ran toward the soccer field. "And besides, I need a new excuse for being late all the time!"

Pam rolled her eyes and yelled to make sure Angie could hear, "Mom, in that case you'll have to have twins!"

After a victorious game, the Denney family celebrated at their favorite pizza parlor. Michael raised his glass of root beer and proposed a toast. "Here's to the beginning of chapter 2 in the Denney family saga!"

Pam and Angie raised their glasses in unison, "Hear, hear!" Sarah laughed at her adorable family as her glass met the three others. "And let's hope chapter 2 will be at least half as much fun as chapter 1 has been!"

What has been one of the most surprising blessings of your little one?

_____

_____

_____

_____

_____

_____

_____

_____

_____

_____

_____

_____

_____

_____

_____

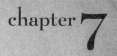

a new mom's
prayer

*W*hen life gets tough,
I am your *hiding* place.
I'm near when you call upon Me in truth.
I'll *protect* you from trouble,
surrounding you with *songs* of deliverance.

*G*ive Me all your worries
and watch Me *sustain* you and your family.
No matter how **bleak** things may seem,
I'll never let the *righteous* fall.
And never doubt that your earnest **prayers**
as a righteous mom are **powerful** and *effective.*

Victoriously,
Your Eternal God of Refuge

—from Psalms 32:7; 145:18; 55:22; James 5:16

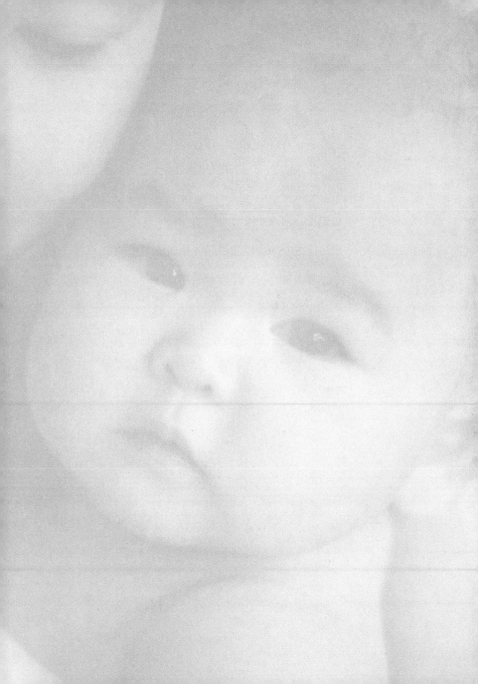

What kind of mother are you? Are you the laid-back mom who doesn't keep track of diaper changes or how long it's been since your baby's last feeding? Or are you the extremely organized mother who has very detailed charts of your child's hour-by-hour activity? Or maybe you're somewhere in-between.

No matter what style of mothering you have chosen, all mothers have one thing in common: the strong sense of love they have for their babies. We've all heard stories of a mother who lifted a car to save her child's life or risked her own life to give birth to the child in her womb. There is something inside every mother that produces an intense desire to protect her young. But what happens when there is nothing you can physically do to protect your child? When illness or disaster puts life out of your control? You do the best thing a mother can do. You pray. You pray that the One who gave you your precious child will protect her in miraculous ways. You ask that your child always be wrapped in the arms of the Savior, especially when your arms are out of reach.

But don't wait until disaster strikes to pray. Start praying for protection for your child right now. Pray for your child's health. Pray for her safety. Pray for her salvation. While you're at it, you may also want to say a prayer of thanks.

Prayer turns your heart
into a vessel
of His love and discernment.
~Pam Farrel

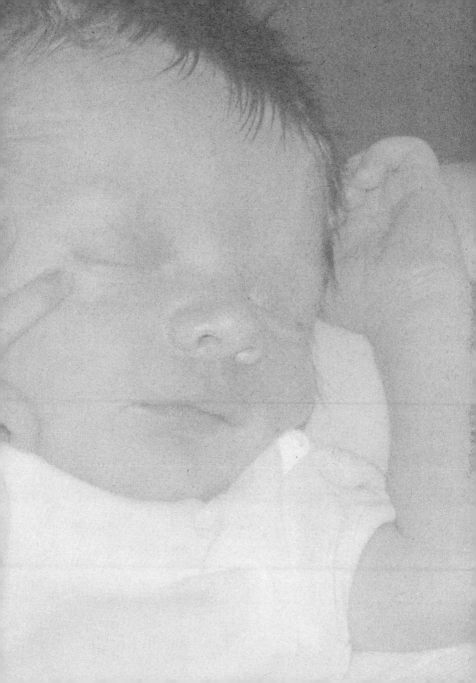

who's in control?

She couldn't decide which was better—the soothing sound of the waves hitting the sand or the warm gulf breeze that gently blew her hair. *But then again, making a decision isn't a priority right now,* Robyn reminded herself as she rolled onto her stomach to even out her tan. Robyn and Dan were taking their first little vacation alone together since five-month-old Saylor had been born. Despite the stress of the previous week—juggling her roles as sales manager, wife, mother, housekeeper, and all those other titleless jobs—she was determined to enjoy this weekend trip. Even the four-hour drive to the beach was a treat because it had been a long time since she and Dan had shared a conversation without tending to Saylor.

Dan had been so sweet to coordinate this trip all by himself—and without her suspecting a thing! He had reserved a condo, made reservations at a fancy French restaurant, and had even arranged for Robyn's sister, Claire, to keep Saylor for the two nights they would be gone.

"I don't know, Dan," Robyn had protested. "This is the first time we've ever left Saylor overnight!" Robyn, though excited about the trip, felt her motherly instincts kick in as she fretted about leaving their baby.

"Saylor will be just fine," Dan had insisted. "And I know that her cousins are dying to help Claire baby-sit. Besides, we're only four hours away, so if anything were to happen, we could jump right back in the car and come home." Robyn hadn't needed too much persuasion because the idea of sleeping in was almost enough in itself!

And so far, the weekend had been wonderful. Walking on the beach, soaking up some sun, fine dining, and uninterrupted sleep had been almost too enjoyable! It had been incredible until they heard Dan's cell phone ring. "Hi, guys. It's Claire. I don't want to worry you, but Saylor has a little fever. I gave her some Children's Tylenol, so I'm sure her temperature will go down, but I just wanted to let you know. Saylor is having a ball playing with the kids, but she may be coming down with something. I'll keep you posted, so don't change your plans. I'll call you in the morning to let you know how she's doing."

Robyn was a little more than worried. "Dan, should we go home? What if Saylor gets worse?"

Dan, ever the epitome of calm, tried to soothe his wife. "Relax, sweetie. You heard Claire. Saylor is having a good time; she's just running a little fever. Let's wait until the morning. If we left right now, we still wouldn't be home before midnight, and Saylor would be asleep anyway." Dan could see the tension in

Robyn's face as he put his arms around her. "But if it would make you feel better, we can leave right now."

Robyn relaxed slightly in his strong arms. "No, I guess you're right. We might as well get some sleep tonight, but I'll call Claire first thing in the morning."

Morning came a little sooner than expected when Claire called at 4:30 A.M. "Saylor's fever is 101, and her breathing is labored and irregular. I'm on my way to the emergency room. I'll call you back as soon as I know something."

Dan and Robyn tried to stay within a reasonable range above the speed limit as they flew down the highway. With a furrowed brow, Dan kept his eyes on the road, one hand on the wheel and his other hand attempting to steady the trembling hands of Robyn.

"Oh, Dan, I hope she's OK. What could have happened? She was fine before we left! What will the doctors do to her? I feel so helpless!"

"Just keep praying, honey. That's all we can do right now," Dan said quietly.

When they arrived at the hospital, Claire was talking to the doctor outside Saylor's room. "Oh, here they are, Dr. Stanley." Dr. Stanley was a tall, broad man in his late forties with a gentle smile.

"I was just telling Claire what we have done so far. We are running the blood work to see if this is viral or bacterial. We really don't know what we are dealing with, but Saylor's temperature is staying pretty high, and she is having a hard time breathing on her own. We have her on an IV, and we're giving her an antibiotic until we can rule out infection. She is receiving oxygen from the plastic tent that surrounds the bed. Until we get the results of the tests, she will be under observation. You can go in now."

Robyn was not prepared for what she saw. She covered her mouth as she let out a gasp at the sight of her precious baby under the oxygen tent. Her miniature body lay limp while her chest lowered and raised heavily. She saw that Saylor's left leg was completely bandaged to secure the IV that had been attached to her foot. Saylor's little lips were blue-tinged; and if Robyn hadn't known better, she would have said that this wasn't her baby. She looked so pitiful lying on the big hospital bed. Although Robyn had enough self-control not to wail out loud, her heart ached for the listless body they said was her baby girl. As Robyn reached under the tent to caress her daughter's tiny arm, Dan held Robyn's shoulder tightly to make his presence known.

The day seemed to last a week while the doctor ordered test after test, trying to determine what was wrong with Saylor. Saylor slipped in and out of a restless sleep as the nurses gently poked and prodded on her little body.

Robyn and Dan were grateful for the helpfulness of the staff, but their sleeping arrangements were less than luxurious. Dan slept on a pullout sofa, and

Robyn slept in the hospital bed under the tent with little Saylor in her arms. The room was dark except for the bright streetlight that flickered through the closed shade.

As Robyn lay there in the quiet, listening to the occasional sounds of the oxygen whirring, she prayed like she'd never prayed before. "Dear Father, I would do anything to trade places with my little baby right now if only I could. I feel so helpless and realize that I have no control over this situation. All I know to do is to give this completely to You and have faith that Your plan is divine." With tears streaming down her face, she continued, "I praise You for blessing me with this beautiful child, and I thank You for giving me a glimpse of the love I know You have for all of Your children. Right now I ask that You return little Saylor's body back to full health and that we will have the joy of raising her to be a woman of God. But if that is not Your will," she paused to catch her breath between sobs, "I know, dear Father, that You would do a much better job of taking care of her than I could ever do, so I submit myself to Your will." As she completed her prayer, Robyn was finally able to drift into a restful sleep.

The next morning Dr. Stanley made his rounds early. "Well, it appears that whatever Saylor was experiencing was bacterial. Her fever has gone down, and the antibiotics are beginning to do their job. From what I see, we can discontinue the oxygen unless something changes. We need to keep her here for another day, but if she continues to progress, she should be discharged tomorrow morning."

With much relief, Robyn and Dan took turns holding Saylor, who already seemed to have regained quite a bit of strength. Robyn thanked the doctor for all his help and then turned to Dan. "You know, Dan, I've learned a lot through this terrible ordeal. I realize that I don't have as much control over my life and my family as I thought I did. And I'm actually better for knowing it. I am so relieved to let God be in control. I'm going to appreciate what I have and be thankful for the blessing of motherhood along with the joys of loving our child."

With Saylor in one arm and the other wrapped around his amazing wife, Dan looked into Robyn's eyes and said, "I'm feeling pretty thankful too."

Write the story of a difficult time
that taught you to trust God more.

_____

_____

_____

_____

_____

_____

_____

_____

_____

_____

_____

_____

_____

_____